ALGOSAIBI, GHAZI

DUSTING THE COLOUR FROM ROSES/Bilingual edn.

Dusting the Co

Ghazi Algosaibi

Dusting the Colour from Roses

A Bilingual Collection of Arabic Poetry

Translated from the Arabic by A. A. Ruffai
Revised by Heather Lawton

Echoes

British Library Cataloguing-in-Publication Data
A catalogue record for this book is available from
the British Library

ISBN 1 873395 35 3 Hb
ISBN 1 873395 01 9 Pbk

This edition first published 1995 by
Echoes
26 Westbourne Grove
London W2 5RH

Typeset by Group E, London

Contents

The Poems

واللون عن الأوراد

الشَّبَقُ الخريَفي يَمسُّ الشَجَرا
ويُجِبلُ الآفاقَ بالريحِ.. وبالرعدِ.. وبالسوادْ
ويتمادى.. فيذوقُ البَشَرا
وتُرعشُ القلوبُ.. بالخوفِ من المُوتِ..
وبالشوْقِ الى الميلادْ

كنتُ أنا
في الغابةِ السوداءِ أحْدو الضَجَرا

Dusting the Colour from Roses

Autumn's lust touches
trees, impregnating
horizons with gales,
storms and darkness.

Autumn moves further –
tastes humans,
causing hearts to shiver
with the fear of death
And the longing to be born.

Meanwhile I stood in the black forest
nursing ennui, and watching as horizons

وأرقبُ الآفاقَ تنجبُ الأولادْ

سيّدتي!

سيّدتي!

يا مَوسمَ الصيفِ عليّ انفجرا

في غيْبة الميعادْ

رأيتُ في عَينيْكِ

يا لروعة الأضدادْ

رأيتُ بدراً مُبحرا

رأيت بحراً مُقمِرا

سمعتُ كلّ اغنياتِ الغوْصِ..

والرُعاةِ.. والحصادْ

ثانيةً..

وجّرَكِ الصيفُ إليْه.. فانبرى

له الخَريفُ.. جّرني السُهْادْ

struggled to give birth to children.

My lady,
My lady,
O summer which flamed upon me
out of season. In your eyes I saw
(what a splendid paradox) a full moon
sailing across a sea gleaming like the moon.

I heard all the songs of the pearl-
divers and the shepherds; as summer
drags you, once more, towards the harvest,
(And I, insomniac, am dragged along behind.)

سيّدتي!

سيّدتي!

أغنيتي مؤلِمةٌ

نشيجُها يُزعجُ هذا الوَترا

فيشعلُ النيران في الأعوادْ

كأنها أنشودةُ السّيابِ..

ناجَى المطَرا

أو شَهقَاتُ المِلكِ الضّليلِ

في الوِهادْ

أو صَرخَاتُ المتنبّي وهو يُلقي العُمُرا

والخيْلَ.. والليْلَ.. على الأوغادْ

أو دمعُ ناجي وهو يبكي الحجَرا

ويصبغُ الأطلال بالرَمادْ

My lady, .
My lady, .
My song is painful.
My sobs disturb the strings
of the lutes, making the music ignite.
As in the Ode of as-Sayyab, when he cried alone
in the rain;
or the cries of al-Mutanabbi, as he threw
his life into the night,
over the villain's horses,
or the tears of Naji
as he lamented the stones
painting ruins with ashes.

سيّدتي!

سيّدتي!

أُغنيتي

عذابُ كلّ شاعرٍ

عبر القُرونِ.. شَعَرَا

ومَات قبلَ الوصْلِ..

في مفاوز البعادْ

سيّدتي!

سيّدتي!

من الذي أرجَفَ؟

من قال الخريفُ انتحرا؟

من الذي استأجر في جريدةٍ

صفحتها الأولى.. ولفّ النعْيَ بالسَوادْ ؟

تأمّليه.. سَيْطَرا

فلم يَدْع في الغابةِ الخَضراءِ..

إلّا ذكرياتِ الأخضرِ المَيّادْ

My lady,
My lady,
My song is the cry
of every poet transcending
centuries with his poetry,
only to die alone,
a stranger in the desert.

My lady,
My lady,
Who placed an obituary
outlined in black
on the first page of a newspaper
to inform us that autumn
had committed suicide?

Just think about it, lady,
what if autumn took over everything
leaving nothing but memories in the forest
of green plants on their knees?

تأمّليه.. انهمرا
فنفّض الصَيفَ عن الشّباكِ..
واللَون عن الأورادْ
هو الخريفُ سيّد الفصولْ
يحمل أُسرار البقاء والنفادْ
والموتِ والمعادْ

١٩٩٣

Just contemplate autumn draining
summer from windows;
dusting the colour from roses.
It is autumn, the lord of all seasons,
bearing secrets of survival and loss;
of death and of resurrection.

1993

"فاكس"

أنتِ لا تَنشُقين شَذَى النارِ..
إنْ أنتِ راقبْتِها مِنْ بعيدْ
أو عَبير الفؤادِ.. إذا أنتِ
أسكنتِه في قميصِ الحديدْ
أنتِ لا تنشُقين الوُرودَ إذا
خِفتِ من شوكِهٍ في الوريدْ
رُبّما
كنتِ أرْوعَ من قطراتِ النَدى..
وشُعاعِ القَمَرْ

Fax

You cannot smell the fragrance
of the fire
watching it from afar;
or the perfume of the heart
if you imprison it
beneath an iron shirt.
You do not sniff roses
if you fear
a thorn pricking a vein.

Maybe your beauty transcends
the dew
and the moonlight.

رُبّما

كنتِ لَحنْ اَلسَّمر

وجُنونَ السَحَر

إنّما

أنتِ لا تُبصرين احتفال الشموس..

بنظّارةٍ من جليدْ

لا.. ولا قُبلة النجم للنجمِ..

من كُوّةٍ.. في جناح العبيدْ

رُبّما

كنتِ كُلَّ الذي يُنتظَرْ

إنّما

أنتِ لا تُدركين جُنون الربيعِ..

إذا كنتِ لا تعشقينَ الخَطَرْ

أو غَرام الفراشات.. إن كنتِ

تحتقرينَ السَّفَر

20

Perhaps you were the melody
running through the party,
causing madness at dawn.

But you do not see the festival
of the sun
through snow-spectacles.
Nor do you see a star kiss
another star
through the tiny window
in the slaves' quarter.

You might be all a man desires
but you will never comprehend
the madness of spring
if you refuse
to take risks.
Nor will you comprehend
the passion of butterflies
if you hate travel;

أو هِيام الـخِيامِ.. إذا كُنتِ من

ساكناتِ الحَضرْ

رُبّما

كنتِ أفتَن من كل فاتنةٍ..

في الوجودِ الـمَديدْ

إنّما..

أنتِ لا تعرفينَ الحياةَ..

إذا عِشتها بالبريدْ

١٩٩٢

nor one's love for tents
if you insist on
being a city-dweller.
You may be more beautiful
than all the beauties
in the entire universe.
Yet you will never know
life if you continue
to live it via the mail.

1992

أتجعلني جدّاً؟

(عندما رزقت ابنة الشاعر يارا وزوجها فواز القصيبي مولودهما فهد .)

أقولُ لفهْدٍ.. حينَ طالَعَني فَهدُ

"أتجعلني جدّاً؟!" فِداءٌ لك الجدُّ

أتجعلني جدّاً.. وكنتُ أنا الفتى

تُجنَّ به ليلى.. وتعشقه دعد؟

أتجعلني جدّاً.. وكَانتْ قصائدي

ورودَ خدودٍ يشتهي لوْنَها الوردُ؟

أتجعلني جدّاً.. وكَانتْ رسائلي

سَوادَ عيونٍ بعضُ عُشاقِها السُهدُ؟

Are You Making Me a Grandfather?

(On the occasion of the birth of a son, Fahd, to the poet's daughter, Yara, and to her husband, Fawwaz Algosaibi.)

I said to Fahd
When he first looked at me

Are you making me a grandfather?
I, who was doted on by Leila and loved by Daad.

Are you making me a grandfather?
I, whose poems were roses of such depth of hue,
    roses were jealous.

Are you making me a grandfather?
I, whose letters were as sloe-black as their
    admirers' sleepless eyes.

أتجعلني جدّاً.. وأيُّ مليحةٍ
تهيمُ بجدٍ؟ لا سُعادٌ.. ولا هِندُ
سلامٌ على الآرام يرتعن في الصِبا
سلامٌ من الجدِّ الذي إحتازه الـجِدُ

ويا مرحباً يا فهدُ بالقادم الذي
أطلَّ على الدنيا.. كما يشرقُ الوعدُ
أتيتَ بأعراسِ البراءةِ نسمةً
من الحُبّ.. في دنياً يظللُها الحِقدُ
رأيتُك في المهدِ المُعطّرِ..دُميةً
يكادُ من التَحنانِ يلثُمها المهدُ

You dare to make me a grandfather?
Tell me, what beauty would fall in love with a
grandfather?

Surely neither Suad nor Hind – healthy white
antelopes
Frolicking in their youth.

Welcome to Fahd, the new-born who surveys the
world
Coming like a shining promise.

You have brought with you a celebration of
innocence,
A gentle breeze of love, in a world polluted by
hatred.

I saw you in your sweet cradle . . . you were like a
doll
Being rocked by the cradle, in a display of
tenderness.

ففاضتْ جفوني بالرؤى.. وتَراقصتْ
أمامي طيوفُ الأمسِ.. تبدو ولا تبدو
أأمُك هذي؟! تلك يارا صغيرتي
على كتفي تحبو.. وفي أضلعي تعدو
أكادُ أراها بين قلبى.. وأمّها
يهشّ لها ثغرُ.. ويحرسها زَندُ
سجدتُ لربّي حين أبصرتُ طفلها
لَه الحمدُ.. كم أغنى وأقنى.. له الحمد!

١٩٩٣

I wept then, lost in a vision of the past,
Its spectres appearing only to disappear again.

Was that your mother – my little Yara?
Clambering over my shoulder, running across my
    chest . . .
Nestling between my heart and her mother's,
Guarding with a forceful arm her chortling, tiny
    mouth.

When I saw Yara's baby first I knelt before God.
Praise be to Him who gives and cares.

To Him
Be Praise.

1993

في الشارع القديم

نعود إليهِ
إلى شارعٍ كان منزلُنا ذات يومٍ
يطلُّ عليهِ
ونسأله عن سنينِ هوانا
فيأتلقُ الشوقُ في شفتيْهِ
ونسأله عن سنين صِبانا
فيحترقُ الدمعُ في ناظريْهِ

مضى رُبع قرنٍ.. واكثرْ

In the Old Street

We return
   To the street which long ago
Our home overlooked.

We ask it
   About the years of our love.
And longing glistens on its lips.

We ask it
   About those years when we were young.
And its eyes burn with tears.

A quarter of a century or more has passed.

تغيّر ذاك الفتى.. وتغيّرَ..
ثُمَّ تغيّرْ
فقد كان أنقى.. وأبهى.. وأشعرْ
أغار بخنجره في صدور المعاركِ..
حتّى وهى.. وتكسّرْ
وأشرع زورقه في عيون العواصف..
حتّى ارتمى.. وتكسّرْ
وطاف بخافقه في الصحاري..
إلى أن تحجّرْ
وعاد يجُر حُطَام السنينْ
ويكتب هذا القصَيد المُكرّرْ

هنا مطعم الأمس..
نفسُ الطعامِ البذيء الغريبْ

And that young man has changed
And changed and changed . . .

Then his mind was pure and brilliant.
    And he was a better poet,
He plunged his dagger into the heart of conflicts.
    Until the dagger broke.
And he sailed his ship fearlessly
    Into the eye of the storm until he drifted and
    was wrecked.

He roamed the deserts with his passionate heart,
    Until that too ossified and
He returned, dragging the ruins of his years behind
    him,

To produce these recycled poems you read.
    See, here is the restaurant of yesterday,
Serving the same obscene food.

هنا بائعُ الكُتْبِ

نفسُ البضاعةِ.. نفسُ الروائحِ..

نفسُ الغُبارْ

وفي المنحنى لا يزال الصِغارْ

بنفسِ الجُنونِ.. ونفسِ الشِجارْ

ومنزلُنا..

كُلّ شيءٍ كما كان..

حتّى الجرائدُ تستبقُ الفجرَ..

حتّى الحليبْ

لماذا نشيبْ

وتبقى الشوارع ليستْ تشيبْ؟

على البابِ..

أُوشك أن ألمسَ الزّرّ..

Here is the bookseller, selling the same old books.
　　Around the corner lies the same dust, the
　　　　same smells
And children, just as crazy and wild as before,
　　playing.

Our house is just the same as it always was –
　　Even down to the daily newspapers
And milk delivered before dawn breaks.

Tell me this – why do men grow old,
　　Old and grey, while the streets remain
The same as they always were, are now, and will
　　be?

Now at the door I am tempted to ring the bell.

ثم يعودُ الزمانْ
ويهوي على كتفي.. ربُع قرنٍ
فأهمسُ، "كانْ
وما عاد منزلَنَا".
كلّ شيء تغيّر.. إلا المكانْ
وإلا عُيونك..
نفسُ الطفولة..
نفسُ البراءة..
نفسُ الحنانْ

Time quickly hovers on my shoulder.
A quarter of a century, I whisper –

It won. This is no longer our home. All has
    changed.
        Except this place and your eyes.
The same childhood here, and tenderness and
    innocence.

زمانٌ عجيبْ!
أأكبر وحدي..
وتبقين أنتِ..
وتبقى عيُونكِ..
تبقى الشوارعُ..
ليستْ تشيبْ؟!

١٩٩٢

This is a strange time, for I alone grow old;
    While you and your eyes and the streets
Stay the same, without growing old and grey.

1992

مهرجان الأسئلة

وُعودٌ في شفاهكِ أَمْ وعيدُ ؟
وتبخلُ، وهي تهمسُ، أم تَجودُ ؟
وحينَ ضحِكتِ.. هَلْ حَيّا لهيبٌ
فداكِ الجمرُ! أَمْ شهقتْ ورودُ ؟
أبنتَ الجنّة الخضراءِ! أنّى
تلاقِينا.. وموعدُنا الحسَودُ؟!

Carnival of Questions

Are these promises
or threats
on your lips?
When you whisper
are your lips mean
or tender?
And when you laugh
were those flames rising
towards me or roses sighing?
O you daughter of green
paradise, when will our jealously
guarded meeting take place?

أراكِ مع الحُشودِ..فهل تراني
أنا مْن تبصرينَ.. أمِ الحشُود؟
وحْولكِ كلُ ما تهبُ الأماني:
جمالُك.. والشبابُ.. وما يريدُ
وحوْلي.. كُلّ ما تلدُ المآسي:
خريفُ العمر.. والقلبُ الشهيدُ
وقافيةٌ.. كما يجري وتينٌ
وأغنيةٌ.. كما فُتح الوريدُ

هفا.. فرنا.. فضجّ.. فثَار.. شوقٌ
سليبُ الكبرِ.. ذو خجلٍ.. عنيدُ
يؤرّقُه الوِصالُ.. ولا وِصالٌ
ويقتلُه الصُدودُ.. ولا صُدودُ
ألا عجباً لطفلٍ صَار كهلاً
يعبّ من الجنونِ.. ويستزيدُ

In the midst of the crowd
I catch sight of you; but is it I
you are looking at or other people?

All you could possibly desire
lies around you – your beauty
and your youth with all its longings . . .
While around me lie the trappings
of tragedy . . . I am in the autumn
of life, bearing a martyred heart;
rhymes and songs bleeding from severed
veins. I longed, so I gazed and my desire
rose and beat a loud note.

I am usurped by age.
Shy and stubborn, I am rendered sleepless
by imagining communication when there is none;
by dying from rejection – when there is none.
How strange for a child to grow old,
swallowing folly and demanding more.

أُكفكفُ ما تناثر من حنيني
فيخذلني.. ويخذله.. الصمودُ
وأزعم أن ما ألقاه وهمٌ
أوهمٌ ذاك.. أمْ خَصرٌ وحيدُ ؟
وأنتِ كغيْمةٍ.. حَبلتْ بسّرٍ
أغيثٌ ما تدبّرُ.. أمْ رعودُ ؟

أتيتُكِ من تباريح الصحارى
أساريري الشواهقُ.. والنجودُ
وأحلامي الأراكةُ والخَزامَى
وأيامي القوافلُ.. والبريدُ
وفجري كُلَّ ما ناجاه ليلٌ
وليلي كُل ما غنّاهُ عُودُ
عطُور العامريّة.. في ثيابي
وقيسٌ.. والحطيئةُ.. والشريدُ

In vain I try to control my dispersed
desires, by maintaining that I see
an illusion. But was the outline
of your waist and neck a dream?
And you who conceived a plan so secretly
are like a cloud, and I know not
whether you will bring rain or thunderstorms.

I come to you from the emotional torrents of
        deserts.
My features are heights and lowlands.
My dreams are of desert bushes and lavender.
My days are caravans and mail.
My dawn is composed of words whispered to a
        love at night;
and my night is composed of songs accompanying
        the lute.
My clothes are scented with the perfume of al-
        Amiriyah,
Qais, Hutai'ah and al-Shareed.

فماذا تأمرين؟.. وما تبقّى
من الأيام منتشرٌ بديدُ؟

١٩٩٢

So what are your orders?
The remains of my days are for you to scatter and
   waste.

1992
———————————

ماذا أقول؟

أتعودُ يَا زمَن الطُفولةْ؟!
أتعودُ للصبّ الذي
ناداك.. وهو يجوزُ آثامَ
الشبابِ إلى حماقاتِ الكهولهْ
متأرجح الخطوَاتِ.. ما بين السلامة..
والنَدامة.. والصعوبةِ
والسُهولهْ؟
أتعود يا زمَن الأساطيرِ..
المُلونَة الحكايا؟

What Am I to Say?

Childhood,
Are you coming again? Are you returning
To the lover calling you in transit?

Between the sins of his youth and the follies
Of old age; his steps swinging between
Security and regret, difficulty and ease.

O Time
Of myth and colourful stories
Are you coming back?

أتعودُ يا زمنَ التنقُّلِ

في المدائنِ.. والتغرُّبِ

في الصَّبايا؟

أتعودُ للصَب الذي..

حَسَب الشجاعة في الهزيمةِ..

والرُّجولة في الفُحولهْ؟

أتعود لي.. وأنا أفتّش

عن ملامحيَ القديمة.. في

التصاوير القديمة.. والمرايا؟

وأجوب أعماق السفائن والمدائنِ!!

صارخاً: "هاتي صِبايا"!؟

ماذا سأفعلُ بالزهورِ المقُبلاتِ

على الذُبولْ؟

أو بالكواكب وهي تحتضن الأُفولْ؟

أو بالسنين الغاربات.. ولا قُفولْ؟

O Time
Of travel in cities and of loss in young girls
Are you coming back?

Are you coming back
To the lover who saw courage in defeat
And manliness in virility?

Are you coming back
While I scan old photographs and mirrors
For my former features?

And roam the depths of ships and cities
Screaming,
"Give me back my youth."

What am I going to do with the flowers
Which are about to wilt; or with the stars
About to set, or the years passing without return?

لوُ عُدتِ لي..
ماذا أقولْ ؟!

١٩٨٨

And if you come back to me
What am I going to say?

1988

في أصابع الخمسين

أوَ ما أنبأوكِ قبل لِقانا

أنّي في أصابع الخمسينا؟!

تأخذ الرُّوح من عروقيَ.. حيناً

وتردّ العروق والروحَ.. حينا

ترسل الشيْب عَبْر شعريَ.. لصاً

يتوقّى، شأن اللصوص، كمينا

قطف الأسود النضير.. شَمالاً

In the Grip of My Fifties

Did they not tell you,
Before we met,
That I am in the grip
Of my fifties?
Years which drain me of spirit
and life-blood sometimes;
And at other times capriciously
Renew both body and soul.

Those same ambushing years
Who steal the jet-black hairs
From the left side of my head;

وتمشّي يمحو السوادَ.. يمينا

أو ما أنبأوكِ أني حِصانٌ

عاد من لُجةِ الحروبِ طعينا؟

أمطرتْ ظهَره الرماحُ دماءً

يا لروضٍ يحسُو نَجيعاً هَتونا

أو ما أنبأوكِ أنّي غريقٌ

أحرقوا البَحر، خلفه، والسفينا؟

أو ما أنبأوكِ أنّيَ كهلٌ

يرقبُ المغرب الحزين.. حزينا؟

يرمق الشمس ليس يدري.. أتبقى

لحظةً ثم ترتمي أم سنينا

Whilst destroying all blackness
From the right side.

Did they forget to tell you
That I resemble a horse
Returning, broken and bleeding,
From the battlefield where javelins
Rained upon my back?

O garden, sipping blood,
Pouring like rain,
Didn't they tell . . .
That I am a drowning man
Behind whom they've burnt
Both the boats and the sea?
Have they not told you
That I am middle-aged,
Surveying the sad evening,
Staring at the setting sun
In sorrow – knowing not
If it would stay for a moment
Or for years before sinking?

كنتُ يا طفلتي الشهيّةَ.. يوماً
سيّد المغرمين.. والعاشقينا
كنتُ ان تلمسِ الضفيرةُ قلبي
يهطلُ الشعرُ فوقها ياسمينا
كان محّارةَ الحِسان.. فؤادِ
يتزاحَمْنَ لؤلؤاً مكنونا
قبل أن ترحلَ الثلاثون عنّي
وتسوقُ الصبيّ للأربعينا
قبل أن تُقبل السنين اللواتي
تأكلُ الشعرَ.. والصبا.. والجُنونا

My delicious child,
Once upon a time,
I was the lord
Of lovers and the beloved.
My heart had only to be touched
By a woman's plaited hair
For poetry to entwine it like jasmine.

My heart was an oyster
Where beautiful women,
Like hidden pearls,
Crushed close against the other.

That was in my thirties,
Before youth dragged me
Forward into my forties.
Before the passing of years,
Devouring my hair, youth and madness.

فلماذا قَدِمْتِ في فوْرة العمر

جمالاً.. مُدللاً.. مفتونا؟

ولماذا أشرقتِ.. بسمةَ شوقٍ؟

من رأى بسمةً تشبُّ أتونا؟

من رأى بسمةً رَمتْ نِصفَ قرنٍ

فأعادته من جديدٍ.. جنينا؟

١٩٩٠

Why have you come now
In the prime of your youth,
Beauty and flirtatiousness?
And why did you shine
A smile of longing?
Whoever saw a smile dazzling in fire?
Whoever saw a smile transcending
Half a century
To bring him back again
As a baby?

1990

الصقر.. والمستحيل

وكالحُلْم جئتِ.. وكالحُلْم غبتِ
وأصبحتُ أنفضُ منكِ اليَدَا
فما كان أغربَه.. مُلتقىً
وماكان أقصره.. موعدا

The Falcon and the Impossible

As if in a dream
        You appeared
And disappeared.
        So, looking at my hands
I did not
        Find you there.
What a strange meeting
        Such a short date.

رأيتُك.. والجْمعُ ما بيننا

فلم أر غيْركِ.. عبْر المَدَى

شِفاةٌ كما يتحدّى الربيعُ

وجَفنٌ كما تتعرّى المُدى

فيَالكِ منَ وردةٍ أُرهِقتْ

بحوْمِ الفراش.. وسَقطِ الندى

I saw you first
   When the crowds were
Between us.
   But across the distance
I could see
   You were unlike
    Any other.

With lips reminiscent of spring;
   Eyes naked
As a knife-blade,
   You are a rose,
Drained by butterflies
   Flirting
And the oppression of falling
   Dewdrops.

ويا ليَ من شاعرٍ عاشقٍ
ينادي الهوى.. فيخوضُ الردى
ويتلو عليك.. عيون القصيدِ
ويرقب عينيكِ.. يَرجو الصدى
كطفلٍ يداهن أستاذه
ليهمَسَ "أحسنت!".."ما أجودا!"
ويطرقُ أستاذهُ واجماً..
ولا يذكر الطفلُ ما أنشدا
ولا تنظُرين.. ولا تَنطقينَ
وأرجع مُستسلماً.. مُجهدا

You see before you a devoted poet:
　　　His love calls
　　And he charges headlong
Into the battle-lines
　　　Reciting madly
　　Aloud to you
The best of his poetry,
　　　Scanning your eyes,
Desperate for a response.

Just as a child
　　　Longs for his teacher
　　To say, "Well done, wonderful",
But the teacher would be silent
　　　And the child's mind
　　A blank.
So you turn away, saying nothing,
　　And I return shattered,
　　　Suffering.

إذن جُنَّ مَن قبليَ الشعراء
وما كنتُ في الـصّبوة الأوحدا
ولَم يبقَ من طائرٍ ما شدا
ولا وترٍ لكِ ما غرّدا
إذن أنا أقبلتَ أُهدي التمور
لهَجرٍ.. وأرقبُ منها الجَدا !

أيا ابنة كلٍّ اخضرار المروج
أنا ابن الجفافِ.. وما استولّدا
ويا ابنة كلٍ مياهِ الغمام
أنا طفلُ كلٍ قرون الصدى

I must remember
Poets have been driven mad before.
        I am inclined to imagine
        Birds sing just for you
And that strings are plucked just for you.
        I am not the only one in love and
Offering up dates as a gift to Hajr,
        Praying for blessings.

    O daughter
Of all the greenest pastures,
    I am the son
        of drought.
    O daughter
Of all the rainfall in the clouds,
    I am the child
Of centuries of thirst.

ويا كُلَّ أفراحِ كلّ الطيورِ
أنا كُل أحزانِ مَنْ قُيّدا
دموعُ الجموعِ.. علَّى ناظريّ
وذلُّ اليتامَى.. وخَوفُ العِدا
عرفتُ عُصارة كُل الهمومِ
رضيعاً.. وعانيتها أُمردا
وجرَّبتها.. وحسامُ السنين
مشيبٌ على مفرقي عَربدا
فمالكِ.. يا دُمية المُترفين..
تثيرين هذا الأسى الأربدا؟
ومالكِ يا نشْوةَ القادرينَ
تهزّين في يأسه المُقعدا ؟

70

O delight
Of all feathered birds of the air,
    I bear all the sorrows of those in cages.
        My eyes hold the tears of the crowd,
The humiliation of the orphans,
The fear of the enemy.

    As a babe
I have suckled the milk of this world's pain.
    As an adolescent
I bore its angst on my young shoulders.
    As a man
with the sword of time cutting swathes
through my silver hair, I still suffer.

    You, a doll of luxury,
Why stir up the ashes of my sadness?
    Why do you, who can entwine the able in
ecstasy?
Why do you come to haunt this crippled spectre?
    Why me?

سلامٌ عليكِ!.. على العاشقينَ
يضُمهمُ الليل في المنتدى
على كلّ من ذَاقَ.. أو لم يذقْ
على كُلّ من رَاح.. أو مَن غدا
سلامٌ عليكِ.. على لحظةٍ
من العُمرِ.. أعطيتُها المِقودا
فطارتْ الى شُرُفات الجنونِ
الى حيث يعثُر حتّى الهُدى
وأغرتْ بيَ المُستحيلَ.. اللَذيذَ
فأسلمني الأُفقَ المُوصَدا
فيا حُرقةَ الصقرِ.. شَامَ السُها
فخرّ صريعاً.. وما استُشهدا

Greetings
To all you lovers locked in the night
in the sanctuary of passion.
Greetings
To all who put their lips to the chalice of love,
And those who withdrew into celibacy.
Greetings
To a past time when I told love to lead me
By a golden chain
To the edge of the cliff where madness and sanity
Jostle for a hold, and when even the most
experienced
Guide might fall.

I was urged on,
On to a locked chamber on a far horizon
Seeking impossible delicious mysteries.
And what torture for the falcon.
Looking out always for the skies.
Then to drop dead without even the glory
Of a martyr's death.

غداً تنقشُ الريحُ من ريشه:

"تعيشُ الصقورُ.. وتفنى سُدى!"

١٩٩٢

Tomorrow
    The wind will take one of its feathers
    And engrave the air with the
words:
        "Falcons live
      and
          Falcons die
            in vain."

1992

وداعيّة .. للصيف

(إلى الحسناء.. أوال.)

أشحْ بوجهِكَ.. لا تُظهِرْ لها الألَمَ
واكتمْ دُموعكَ.. أغلى الدمع ما كُتِما
إن الحبيبة إن ودّعتَ مكتئباً
غيرُ الحبيبة إن ودّعْتَ مبتسما
دعِ الأسى لليالٍ بَعد فُرقتِها
لا ترتجي قمراً فيها.. ولا حُلُما

A Farewell to Summer

(A song for Bahrain.)

Turn away your face,
show her no pain.
Hide your tears –
The most precious tears
Are those which do not fall.
A farewell to a lover made
when depressed is not the same
as one made smilingly.
Leave sorrow for nights to come,
nights which no moon
or dream will ever adore.

صيفيّة العين!.. غاب الصيف.. وانصرمْت

أيامُه.. أجملُ العُمر الذي انصرما

يسافرُ الصيفُ في عينيكِ يتركنى

على نيوب خريفٍ لم يَزلْ نَهما

أيرجعُ الصيفُ.. والفَودان من لهبٍ

والقلب صمتُ رمادٍ ودَّع الضَرَما؟

أيرجع الصيفُ.. والخمسونُ مطبقةٌ

عليّ.. لا رحمةً أبدتْ.. ولا ندما؟

You with the summery eyes,
Summer has vanished,
Its long days lapsed.
Our happiest days are past..
In your eyes summer
Lies eternal,
Abandoning me to the jaws
Of autumn – which awaits me
With greed.

Will summer ever return?
Now the temples' hair is aflame,
And the heart, in the silence
Of ashes, which'll never rekindle.
Will summer return
Now that the fifties grip me
With no mercy
With no regret?

ليت الشبابَ كهذا البحرِ.. شيبتُه
تنداحُ في زَبَدٍ.. والقاع مَا علما

ليْتَ الشباب كهذا البْدرِ.. مَفرقةُ
يزدانُ إن ضجّ فيه الشيبُ.. واحتدما

ليت الشبابَ بعمر الحُبِّ.. يا امرأةً
ما زال حُبّي لها طفلاً.. وما فُطما

I wish youth
Resembled the sea
With the sea-bed
Utterly ignorant
Of the grey waves.
I wish youth
Was like the full moon,
The whiter,
The brighter.

I wish youth
Could survive love.
O woman, whoever loves you
Is like an unweaned child.

سمراءُ ! سبعٌ مضت ؟ أم لحظةٌ عبرت؟

أم ذاكَ وهمٌ تـمّناه الذي وهما؟

تجري السنينُ بُروقاً إن طوتْ فَرحَاً

ويزحفُ اليومُ دهراً إن حوى سأما

أقولُ.. والشفةُ اللمياءُ تمنحني

ولا تضنُ.."بروحي أفتدي الكَرمَا!"

لثمتُ برًّا وخُلجاناً.. وأشرعةً

والبدرَ.. والليْلَ.. والسُمّار.. والنَغَمَا

O brunette,
Is it seven years passed or
A moment?
Or an illusion conjured up
By the dreamer?
Years fly like lightning
If they bring pleasure.
And a single day crawls
Into eternity
If it brings boredom.

I say
so long as your kohled lips
give without restraint
"My soul is held ransom
By your generosity."
I kiss land, gulfs, sails,
full moons, night,
evening companions and song.

تغفو شفاهي على النُّعمى..فوا لَهفِي
اذا غفتْ في ظمأً مستنجدٍ بظما

قُصّي عليّ حكايانا.. وأغربُها
ماكان حين استحلّ الجارُ ما حُرما
الغدرُ أوجعُ ما ذُقنا.. وأوجَعُهُ
غدر الشقيق الذي علّمتُه..
أهوى بطعنته النجلاءِ.. فاندفعتْ
ترُشّ وجهي.. وثَوبي.. والطَريقَ دما
وكُنتِ والزيفُ ملءَ الأُفق شامخةً
ما بعتِ يومكِ.. والأجدادَ.. والشِيَما
وكنتُ خَلفك أحدو الريح.. قافيتي

My lips drift
Into a sleep of happiness.
(Too bad if they drifted
parched with a thirst
which could never
be assuaged.)

Speak to me of parables –
Especially the one of the neighbour
seizing that which belongs not to him.
Speak to me of treachery.
The time we became his victims,
when he wounded me in the guts,
showering my face, garments
and path with blood.
And while falsehood trod the horizon
you remained a tower of faith,
never betraying yourself
or your forefathers.
I was standing behind you,
begging the wind
to whirl forward.

رصاصتي.. رُبّ شِعرٍ ضِيَم فانتقما

يدنو الفراقُ كذئبٍ جائعٍ حذرٍ
إذا رأى غِرّةً من خصمه هجما
وخِصمُه حَمَلٌ.. يجتاحُه.. وَجَلّ
لو أُبْصَر الذئبَ في أحلامِهِ جثما
يدنو الفراق.. فقولي كيفَ أدفعه
أيدفع الخوفُ مقدوراً إذا اقتحما؟
لو يعرف الذئب ما ألقاه.. أمهلني
وهل سمعتِ بذئبٍ جائعٍ رَحَما؟

Rhyme is my bullet
And poetry my gun –
(for poetry betrayed is vengeful).

Like a hungry, yet cautious wolf
the moment of our parting nears.
And the wolf, scenting fear,
Pounces upon his enemy,
who is gentle as a lamb
and just as terrified,
and on seeing the wolf in his dream
he cowers. Yet the moment is coming
closer when we must part.

Tell me how to stop it,
how to change our destiny.
If the wolf knew my travails
he would have shown me compassion.
But have you heard of the wolf
Showing compassion to the meek lamb?

أتذكرين إذا ما غبتُ في سَفَري
أني خلعتُ على عينيْكِ سِحرهما؟!
وأنني قلتُ في عينيكِ قافيةً
ما استوْطَنت ورقاً لولايَ أو قلما؟
وأنني كنتُ في العُشاق.. أعشَقَهُمْ
وكنتُ في الشعراءِ المُفردَ العَلما؟
وكنتِ بين حبيباتي الأعفّ هوىً
الأجمَلَ.. الأنبلَ.. الأصفى.. الأرقّ فما؟
شِعري كحُسْنِكِ لا يَخبُو شبابُهما
لم تشكُ ليلى ولا مجنونُها هَرَما

١٩٩٢

When I am away on my travels,
do you remember
that it is I who give
your eyes enchantment?
It is those eyes
I have enshrined
in the light of my poems.
Will you remember that?
And that it was I
who was so dedicated to you?
I, who am unique,
The most outstanding of poets.
You, who were the most virtuous
Among my lovers
And pure and beautiful
and noble and tender.
My poetry is like your beauty –
Its youth will never go out.
For, remember, neither Leila
Nor her mad lover grew old.

1992

أقول له؟!

أقول له..

أم تقولين أنت؟..

لهذا القمر

.. بأنّا كبرنا على الحبّ..

لا نتحمّل حتّى السَهَرْ

وما عاد في وُسعِنا أن نعيشَ المُعانَاة..

قَبل الشُروقِ.. وبَعْد السَحَرْ

Shall I Tell the Moon?

Shall I tell the moon
– or shall you –
That we are too old for love?

Too old to bear late nights,
Too old to live through the suffering
of time before, and time after dawn.

أقولُ لهُ..

أم تقولين أنتِ؟..

"علامَ نُضيّع هذا الشُّعاعَ الجميلَ علينا

ونحنُ نفَضنا يدينا

من الحُب؟ نحن انتهيْنا

من الشوق؟ نحن ارتمينا

على عَتَباتِ الضَجرْ؟"

أقول لهُ..

أم تقولين أنتِ؟..

ولكنه لا يزال يطلُّ.. يضيءُ.. يراود.. يُسحِرُ

ماذا تظنِّين أنتِ؟..

أظنّ الخبيثَ انتصرْ!

١٩٩٤

Shall I or you ask the moon
why it expends its brilliant rays
upon you and me, as we've reneged on love?

We have nothing more to do with desire,
for we have stumbled
upon the threshold of boredom.

Who tells the moon – you or I?
For it continues to watch over us,
incandescent, flirtatious, spellbinding.

What do you think?
I think
The wicked one has triumphed.

1994

أيُّنا عاد سالماً؟!

(في ذكرى الصديق قاسم بن محمد القصيبي، رحمه الله.)

أحتمي في ذُرى السنين الخوالي

مِن فُجاءاتِ ما تكُنُّ الليالي

يا أخا العمر.. حين كان شهياً

يتهادى كغادةٍ معطالِ

Which One of Us Returned Safely?

(In memory of my friend,
the late Qasim Ibn Muhammad Algosaibi.)

In the summit
of years past
I take refuge
from the unexpected
events hidden by time.

O brother
at a point in life
when time
was delicious,
striding leisurely,
like an idle beauty.

يا أخا الشعرِ.. حين كانت قَوافيهِ

احتفالاً بالعيْشِ.. بَعد احتفالِ

يا أخا البدرِ.. والنُّجومِ النشَاوى

والمساءِ الذي يُديرُ اللآلي

أفِراقٌ؟.. أما شبعنا فِراقاً

في حياةٍ بخيلةٍ بالوصالِ؟

O brother
of poetry
when its rhymes
were celebration
after celebration
of living.

O brother
of the full moon,
elated stars,
and the evening
strung with pearls;
was that a parting?

But have we not
had our fill of parting?
In a life
too stingy
to offer us a reunion.

أوداعٌ؟.. لكل ليلٍ صباحٌ
غيرُ ليلِ المنيّة القتّالِ

أغمضُ العين.. لا أراك عليلاً
تتلوّى على نيوب الصِلالِ
لا أرى صُفْرَة الرَدى فوق خديّكَ..
وظلُّ الأسى.. وحزّ النِصال
وأرى صاحبي القديم.. فتيّاً
لا يبالي.. أعنفوانٌ يبالي؟
أغمض العين.. أمتطي صَهْوة الحلم..
وبعض الأحلامِ غيرُ خيالٍ

Was that a farewell?
For every night
there is a morning;
save for the murderous
night of dying.

I close my eyes,
but I do not see you in pain
coiled on the grip
of clattered weapons.
I do not see
the yellowness of death
on your cheeks
beneath the shadow of sorrow
and the incision of arrow-heads.

I see my old friend
youthful, carefree.
(Does vigour ever care?)
I close my eyes,
mount the back of dreams
(some dreams are not illusions).

يعبر النيلُ خاطري.. وعلى النيلِ
رفاقُ الصبا.. وانتَ حِيالي
يأخذ الموتُ كُلَّ شيءٍ.. ويعيا
بالغوالي.. من ذكرياتي الغوالي

آهِ يا قاسمُ المُعذَّب بالدنيا، غرامُ
الدنيا افتراسُ الرجالِ
تحتسي من دمائنا ما احتسينا
من طِلاها.. في حانة الأهوالِ

My thoughts cross the Nile
when friends
of early youth
were present
and you were near me.

Death grasps almost everything,
but fails in taking
away my dearest memories.
O Qasim,
the one tortured
by life . . .
A life which loves
to ravish men,
sipping from our blood
whatever we drank
from its draught of elegance
in the tavern
of horrors.

أيُّنا عاد سالماً؟ ذاك مطعونٌ

بفقرٍ.. وذاكَ بالأموالِ

رُبَّما أشهرتْ من المَجدِ سيفاً

فالضحايا مواكبُ الأبطالِ

أيُّنا عاد سالماً؟ نحنُ ما بين

دفينٍ.. ودافنٍ في سجالِ

والحصاد المرير جمرٌ على العينيْنِ

يكوي.. ورنّةُ الأطفالِ

Which one of us
returned safely?
The one pierced
with poverty;
or the one pierced
with riches?
Life may unleash
a sword of glory;
But victims
make the rallies
of heroes.

Which one
of us came back safely?
We are locked
in a struggle
between the sexton
and the buried.

And the bitter harvest
smoulders, burning
embers on the eyes.

آه يا قاسم المُعذّبُ بالناسِ..

وقيلٍ.. "وهلْ سمعتَ؟".. وقالِ

أيُّنا عاد سالماً ؟ بين واشٍ

ومُراءٍ.. وكاذبٍ ختّالِ

أيُّنا عاد سالماً؟.. واقترابٌ

كابتعادٍ.. وصحبةٌ كاعتزالِ

رحمة ا لله أمننا.. فتوسّدْ

راحة الأمن بعد رعب القتالِ

١٩٩٣

O Qasim,
the one tortured
by people and
by gossip.
Which one of us returned safely
Amid the informers,
the hypocrites,
the deceitful liars?
Which of us returned safely?
Proximity equals
remoteness;
and company,
solitude.
Our tranquillity
is the mercy of God.
Take comfort in it
after the horror of the fight.

1993

البحر.. والنسيم

أتدرين كيف يمرّ النسيمُ

على وجنة البحر.. ثم يغيبُ..

ولا يذكر البحر شيئاً..

ففي مهجة البحر تسكن كل الزوابع..

كلُ الأعاصيرِ..

كيف سيذكُر، وهو المُدجَّج بالريح ،

لثْمَ النسيْم؟!

ويمضي النسيْم.. وفي قلبِهِ ينزفُ الجرحُ..

The Sea and the Breeze

Do you see how the breeze
Caresses the cheeks
Of the sea, before it leaves,
Without the sea noticing
For in the depths of the sea
Dwell all the hurricanes and storms.
How can the sea, carrying the weight
Of the winds, recollect the kiss
Of the breeze as it passes,
Its wounded heart bleeding?

كم يعشقُ البَحر.. كم ودَّ لو ظلَّ

يلثُم جَبْهته.. ويُغازلُ أمواجه..

ويهيمُ عليهِ...

فيا أنتِ!!...

هل كنتِ حين مررتِ عليَّ

النسيمَ؟..

أم البحرَ؟..

قولي لقلبي الذي بات ينزف منذ اللقاءْ

١٩٩٣

How dearly he loves the sea,
How he longs to stay
Kissing its forehead,
Flirting with its waves.

So, you . . .
Were you the breeze
Or were you the sea
When you passed by me?
Answer to my heart
Which has been bleeding
Ever since our meeting.

1993

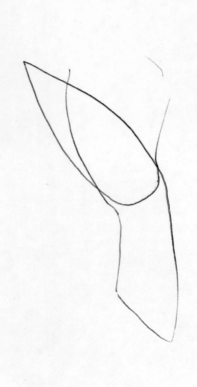